Kerr

SERO SED SERIO

D1178191

Kerr

MOTTO:
Late but in earnest.

CREST:
The sun in his splendour.

TERRITORY:
Roxburghshire.

Kerr

by Iain Gray

Lang**Syne**
PUBLISHING
WRITING *to* REMEMBER

Lang**Syne**

PUBLISHING

WRITING *to* REMEMBER

79 Main Street, Newtongrange,
Midlothian EH22 4NA
Tel: 0131 344 0414   Fax: 0845 075 6085
E-mail: info@lang-syne.co.uk
www.langsyneshop.co.uk

Design by Dorothy Meikle
Printed by Ricoh Print Scotland
© Lang Syne Publishers Ltd 2015

ISBN 978-1-85217-113-1

Chapter one:

Origins of Scottish surnames

by George Forbes

It all began with the Normans.

For it was they who introduced surnames into common usage more than a thousand years ago, initially based on the title of their estates, local villages and chateaux in France to distinguish and identify these landholdings, usually acquired at the point of a bloodstained sword.

Such grand descriptions also helped enhance the prestige of these arrogant warlords and generally glorify their lofty positions high above the humble serfs slaving away below in the pecking order who only had single names, often with Biblical connotations as in Pierre and Jacques.

The only descriptive distinctions among this peasantry concerned their occupations, like Pierre the swineherd or Jacques the ferryman.

The Normans themselves were originally Vikings (or Northmen) who raided, colonised and eventually settled down around the French coastline.

They had sailed up the Seine in their long-boats in 900AD under their ferocious leader Rollo and ruled the roost in north east France before sailing over to conquer England, bringing their relatively new tradition of having surnames with them.

It took another hundred years for the Normans to percolate northwards and surnames did not begin to appear in Scotland until the thirteenth century.

These adventurous knights brought an aura of chivalry with them and it was said no damsel of any distinction would marry a man unless he had at least two names.

The family names included that of Scotland's great hero Robert De Brus and his compatriots were warriors from families like the De Morevils, De Umphravils, De Berkelais, De Quincis, De Viponts and De Vaux.

As the knights settled the boundaries of

their vast estates, they took territorial names, as in Hamilton, Moray, Crawford, Cunningham, Dunbar, Ross, Wemyss, Dundas, Galloway, Renfrew, Greenhill, Hazelwood, Sandylands and Church-hill.

Other names, though not with any obvious geographical or topographical features, nevertheless derived from ancient parishes like Douglas, Forbes, Dalyell and Guthrie.

Other surnames were coined in connection with occupations, castles or legendary deeds. Stuart originated in the word steward, a prestigious post which was an integral part of any large medieval household. The same applied to Cooks, Chamberlains, Constables and Porters.

Borders towns and forts – needed in areas like the Debateable Lands which were constantly fought over by feuding local families – had their own distinctive names; and it was often from them that the resident groups took their communal titles, as in the Grahams of Annandale, the Elliots and Armstrongs of the East Marches, the Scotts and Kerrs of Teviotdale and Eskdale.

Even physical attributes crept into surnames, as in Small, Little and More (the latter being 'beg' in Gaelic), Long or Lang, Stark, Stout, Strong or Strang and even Jolly.

Mieklejohns would have had the strength of several men, while Littlejohn was named after the legendary sidekick of Robin Hood.

Colours got into the act with Black, White, Grey, Brown and Green (Red developed into Reid, Ruddy or Ruddiman). Blue was rare and nobody ever wanted to be associated with yellow.

Pompous worthies took the name Wiseman, Goodman and Goodall.

Words intimating the sons of leading figures were soon affiliated into the language as in Johnson, Adamson, Richardson and Thomson, while the Norman equivalent of Fitz (from the French-Latin 'filius' meaning 'son') cropped up in Fitzmaurice and Fitzgerald.

The prefix 'Mac' was 'son of' in Gaelic and clans often originated with occupations – as in MacNab being sons of the Abbot, MacPherson and MacVicar being sons of the minister and MacIntosh being sons of the chief.

The church's influence could be found in the names Kirk, Clerk, Clarke, Bishop, Friar and Monk. Proctor came from a church official, Singer and Sangster from choristers, Gilchrist and Gillies from Christ's servant, Mitchell, Gilmory and Gilmour from servants of St Michael and Mary, Malcolm from a servant of Columba and Gillespie from a bishop's servant.

The rudimentary medical profession was represented by Barber (a trade which also once included dentistry and surgery) as well as Leech or Leitch.

Businessmen produced Merchants, Mercers, Monypennies, Chapmans, Sellers and Scales, while down at the old village watermill the names that cropped up included Miller, Walker and Fuller.

Other self explanatory trades included Coopers, Brands, Barkers, Tanners, Skinners, Brewsters and Brewers, Tailors, Saddlers, Wrights, Cartwrights, Smiths, Harpers, Joiners, Sawyers, Masons and Plumbers.

Even the scenery was utilised as in Craig, Moor, Hill, Glen, Wood and Forrest.

Rank, whether high or low, took its place with Laird, Barron, Knight, Tennant, Farmer, Husband, Granger, Grieve, Shepherd, Shearer and Fletcher.

The hunt and the chase supplied Hunter, Falconer, Fowler, Fox, Forrester, Archer and Spearman.

The renowned medieval historian Froissart, who eulogised about the romantic deeds of chivalry (and who condemned Scotland as being a poverty stricken wasteland), once sniffily dismissed the peasantry of his native France as the jacquerie (or the jacques-without-names) but it was these same humble folk who ended up overthrowing the arrogant aristocracy.

In the olden days, only the blueblooded knights of antiquity were entitled to full, proper names, both Christian and surnames, but with the passing of time and a more egalitarian, less feudal atmosphere, more respectful and worthy titles spread throughout the populace as a whole.

Echoes of a far distant past can still be found in most names and they can be borne with pride in commemoration of past generations who fought and toiled in some capacity or other to make our nation what it now is, for good or ill.

Chapter two:

Feuds and vendettas

Despite a bitter and bloody feud that raged for more than 300 years between rival branches, the great Borders family of the Kerrs also brought their considerable martial prowess to bear in support of successive Scottish monarchs and, in later centuries, Britain's mighty empire.

It was in recognition of these contributions that the family became the recipients of a plethora of glittering honours, including earldoms and a dukedom.

Numerous derivations have been advanced for the name 'Kerr'. One is that it comes from the Gaelic 'caerr', meaning 'left', and that this relates to a Kerr family trait of being predominantly left-handed.

This, some claim, is where the Scottish expressions 'Kerr-fisted' and 'cori-fisted', to describe someone who is left-handed, originate.

Another possible derivation is from the Gaelic 'ciar', meaning 'dusky', and is said to relate to those Kerrs found on the west coast of Scotland and the island of Arran.

One other colourful derivation, but wholly fabulous, is one that can be traced back to Biblical times, with 'Kerr' in Hebrew being 'Kir'.

In the Brythonic language of the ancient Britons the word for 'fort' was 'caer', and may be another possible derivation of 'Kerr'.

The likeliest derivation, however, is from the Norse word 'kjerr', taken variously to mean copsewood or brushwood, or a marsh dweller.

In the decades following the Norman Conquest of England in 1066, many of the Normans had settled in both England and Scotland.

The Normans, of course, stemmed from the original Vikings, or Norsemen, who settled in France and gave the name of Normandy to the vast province they controlled.

It is probable that one of these Norman families were known by their Norse name of

'Kjerr', and that this was later anglicised as 'Kerr'.

The name, spelled with a single 'r', is first recorded in the Scottish Borders in 1190, and concerns a transaction involving one Johannes Ker, an Anglo-Norman who had settled near the present-day town of Peebles.

Confusingly, over the subsequent centuries, different branches of the Kerrs opted to spell their name with either a single 'r' or two. The name also appears as 'Carr' and 'Carre'.

Two brothers, Ralph and John, are recognised as the founders of the two rival Kerr families that for centuries held sway in the Borders. The main branch was the Kerrs of Ferniehirst, who claimed descent from Ralph, and the Kerrs of Cessford, who claimed descent from John.

Although of the same bloodline, the Kerrs of Ferniehirst and the Kerrs of Cessford were engaged in a virtual civil war with each other until Anne Kerr of Cessford married William Kerr of Ferniehirst in 1631.

It is from this marriage that the Earls and

The stronghold of Ferniehirst

Marquisses of Lothian trace their descent, while the son of Sir William Kerr of Ferniehirst was created the 1st Lord Roxburgh, in 1637.

Following the Act of Union between Scotland and England in 1707, the 5th Earl of Roxburgh was created Duke of Roxburgh.

This title passed in 1805, following a failure in the line with the death of the 3rd Duke of Roxburgh, to Sir James Innes of that Ilk, who took the name of Innes-Ker.

The Marquess of Lothian is today recognised as Chief of the Clan Kerr, while the Duke of Roxburgh is Chief of Clan Innes.

The original source of the bad blood between the Kerrs of Cessford and the Kerrs of Ferniehirst is lost in the mists of time, and when they were not engaged in civil war with one another they were embroiled in deadly disputes with other Border families such as the Armstrongs, Maxwells, Homes, Swintons, Davidsons, Turnbulls, Grahams, Scotts, Douglases, and Elliots.

A bitter feud, for example, had existed

between the Kerrs of Cessford and the Scotts ever since Sir Andrew Kerr of Cessford, who had been one of the few Scots nobles to survive the Battle of Flodden in 1513, had been killed by one of Scott's retainers at a battle near Melrose in 1526.

The Church attempted to broker a resolution to the feud in 1530, by arranging a bond, or agreement, under which Sir Walter Scott of Branxholm, laird of Buccleuch, was obliged to undertake what were known as the four head pilgrimages of Scotland in reparation for the slaying of Kerr of Cessford.

This required that he said a mass for the soul of Cessford at the four locations of Melrose Abbey, Paisley Abbey, Scone Abbey, and the Church of St. Mary, in Dundee.

Sir Walter's pilgrimage of penance failed to heal the rift between the Kerrs and the Scotts, however. A Scott laird of Buccleuch was killed by a Cessford in the streets of Edinburgh in 1552, and despite another attempt made in 1564 to reconcile the two families, they were still at loggerheads until at least as late as 1596.

In the same year, a 20-strong armed band of Turnbulls and Davidsons presented themselves before the Jedburgh residence of Sir Andrew Kerr of Ferniehirst, and after what a contemporary account describes as various 'brags, insolent behaviour and menacings' of Sir Andrew and his servants, they cold-bloodedly killed Sir Andrew's brother, Thomas, and one of his servants.

Although eleven men eventually came to trial, only one Turnbull paid the price when he was beheaded at the Cross of Edinburgh.

In the bloody atmosphere of mafia-style vendettas that then prevailed in the Borders, Turnbull's execution only resulted in further tit-for-tat killings, while the constant feuding made the Borders one of the most wild and unruly parts of the kingdom.

A Privy Council report of 1608 graphically described how the 'wild incests, adulteries, convocation of the lieges, shooting and wearing of hackbuts, pistols, lances, daily bloodshed, oppression, and disobedience in civil matters, neither are nor has been punished.'

Chapter three:

Wardens of the March

**A constant thorn in the flesh of both the
English and Scottish authorities was the cross-
border raiding and pillaging carried out by
well-mounted and heavily armed men, the
contingent from the Scottish side of the border
known and feared as 'moss troopers.'**

In an attempt to bring order to what was
known as the wild 'debateable land' on both sides
of the border, Alexander II of Scotland had in
1237 signed the Treaty of York, which for the first
time established the Scottish border with England
as a line running from the Solway to the Tweed.

On either side of the border there were
three 'marches' or areas of administration, the
West, East, and Middle Marches, and a warden
governed these.

Complaints from either side of the border
were dealt with on Truce Days, when the wardens
of the different marches would act as arbitrators.

There was also a law known as the Hot Trod, that granted anyone who had their livestock stolen the right to pursue the thieves and recover their property.

The post of March Warden was a powerful and lucrative one, with rival families vying for the position. The marches became virtually a law unto themselves.

In the Scottish borderlands, the Homes and Swintons dominated the East March, while the Armstrongs, Maxwells, Johnstones, and Grahams were the rulers of the West March.

The Kerrs, along with the Douglases and Elliots, held sway in the Middle March, and in 1502 a Kerr of Ferniehirst was appointed Warden of the Middle March.

There is no doubt the family abused this influential position, not only at the expense of other Border families, but at the expense of the rival Kerrs of Cessford.

The roles were reversed eleven years later when a Kerr of Cessford was appointed to the post and exacted vengeance against the Kerrs of

Ferniehirst for the abuses they had suffered under their tenure as masters of the Middle March.

This proved to be a pattern that would be repeated in succeeding years as loyalty to the Crown determined which of the Kerrs should hold the post.

The rift between the Ferniehirsts and the Cessfords deepened following the death of James IV at the Battle of Flodden in 1513, and the remarriage of his widow Margaret Tudor to the Douglas Earl of Angus.

In the complex and rapidly shifting loyalties of the time, the Kerrs of Ferniehirst supported the cause of the young James V, while the Cessfords supported Margaret.

In the near anarchy following the death of James IV in 1542, Sir John Kerr of Ferniehirst's castle was taken and occupied by an English force. All the Kerr women and servants were brutally raped by the English garrison.

When the castle was recaptured seven years later, the garrison were tortured before being killed. The incident is the subject of Walter Laidlaw's poem, *The Reprisal*.

The Kerrs of Cessford and the Kerrs of Ferniehurst took opposing sides in the cause of the ill-fated Mary, Queen of Scots, with Sir Thomas Kerr of Ferniehirst fighting for her doomed cause at the Battle of Langside, while Sir Walter Kerr of Cessford fought on the side of the band of nobles supporting the cause of the infant James VI.

Mary had earlier escaped from Lochleven Castle, in which she had been imprisoned after being forced to sign her abdication, by a body known as the Confederate Lords.

Kerr of Ferniehirst was among a group of nine earls, nine bishops, 18 lairds, and others who signed a bond declaring their support for her, and both sides met at Langside, near Glasgow, on May 13, 1568.

Mary's forces, under the command of the Earl of Argyll, had been en route to the mighty bastion of Dumbarton Castle, atop its near inaccessible eminence on Dumbarton Rock, on the Clyde, when it was intercepted by a numerically inferior but tactically superior force led by her half-brother, the Earl of Moray.

Cannon fire had been exchanged between both sides before a force of Argyll's infantry tried to force a passage through to the village of Langside, but they were fired on by a disciplined body of musketeers and forced to retreat as Moray launched a cavalry charge on their confused ranks.

The battle proved disastrous for Mary and signalled the death knell of her cause, with more than 100 of her supporters killed or captured and Mary forced to flee into what she then naively thought would be the protection of England's Queen Elizabeth.

Kerr of Ferniehirst was also forced to flee, and it is testimony to his loyal adherence to Mary that, following his death in 1584, even an English chronicler was moved to write that he had been 'a stout and able warrior, ready for any great attempts and undertakings, and of an immoveable fidelity'.

During the Queen's unhappy time in Scotland, another Kerr, Andrew, played a key role in one of the most brutal incidents in Scotland's murderous history.

The victim was Mary's musician and secretary David Rizzio, who had first come to the Scottish court in 1561 in the train of the Piedmontese ambassador.

Born in Turin, the talented Italian quickly won the favour of the Queen, brightening up the dourness of her court with his musical performances and compositions.

As the Queen's secretary, however, 'Signor Davie' performed a more serious role. Gifted in a number of foreign languages, the Italian helped to draft the secret correspondence between the Queen and what was known as the Catholic League, particularly the Spanish royal court.

This made him highly suspect and dangerous in the eyes of Scotland's Protestant nobles, who feared a concerted conspiracy to overturn the nation's Reformed religion.

Rizzio also flagrantly flouted his favoured position at court, while dark rumours were spread that it was he who was actually the father of the pregnant Queen's child, and not her husband, Lord Darnley, whom she had married in 1565.

The Protestant lords played on the dissolute and gullible Darnley's vicious pride to such an extent that he entered into a bond, or agreement, with them, to solve the problem of the upstart Italian once and for all by arranging for his murder.

The most prominent nobles involved in the drama that was played out on the night of March 9, 1566, were the Lords Ruthven, Murray, Morton, and Lindsay, although they also had the active support of retainers and other Scottish magnates, including Andrew Kerr.

On the night that was to prove the hapless Rizzio's last one on earth, Lord Darnley brought a number of the heavily armed men into his own chamber at the Palace of Holyrood and then led them up a secret stair into his wife, the Queen's, apartments.

It was an innocent scene that greeted the murderous band as they entered one of the Queen's small chambers. Heavily pregnant, she reclined on a low couch, surrounded by a number of loyal retainers and favourites, including Rizzio.

A fierce argument ensued over this unpardonable breach of her privacy and words quickly led to violent deeds as the armed men attempted to wrest the cowering Italian from the chamber.

Clinging to the Queen's gown for protection, he was pulled away, ripping the rich fabric in the process. As he was dragged from the room, pleading and screaming for mercy, Andrew Kerr brutally held a pistol to the Queen's breast to prevent her from going to the doomed Italian's aid.

His pleas for mercy in vain, Rizzio was stabbed and slashed repeatedly with daggers, before his lifeless body was unceremoniously thrown down a flight of stairs into the porter's lodge, where the porter lost no time in stripping the fine clothing from his bloodstained corpse.

Many of those involved in Rizzio's murder, including Andrew Kerr, escaped subsequent punishment, but Lord Darnley himself was murdered in mysterious circumstances just under a year later.

Chapter four:

For Union and Empire

Following the Union of the Crowns of England and Scotland under James VI in 1603, the Kerrs thrived as loyal servants of the Crown, and this attachment was reinforced when the 5th Earl of Roxburgh was created Duke of Roxburgh in recognition for his support for the Act of Union of 1707.

The Act of Union, which united both nations on a political level, is still a controversial subject, with some claiming that those Scottish nobles such as the 5th Earl of Roxburgh who were responsible for the final acceptance of the terms of union gave their support only because they were bribed to do so.

The national bard, Robert Burns, famously described them as a 'parcel of rogues', who were 'bought and sold for English gold.'

With the benefit of hindsight, however, it is possible to discern that the motives of at least some of the nobles were honourable and their actions dictated by what they sincerely believed to be the best interests of Scotland.

Conferment of the dukedom was the culmination of a series of royal favours conferred separately on the Ferniehirst and Cessford branches of the family, and stretching back to at least the 14th century when the head of both branches were honoured with knighthood.

The title of Earl of Roxburgh was first conferred on the Cessfords in 1616, while the 1st (Ferniehirst) Earl of Lothian was created in 1631. A son of the 1st Earl of Lothian was later advanced to the title of Marquess, and also succeeded to the title of Earl of Ancram – another title that had been bestowed on the Kerrs of Ferniehirst.

When Jacobite hopes were dashed forever in the terrible carnage of the Battle of Culloden in April of 1746, two sons of the 3rd Marquess of Lothian fought on the side of the Hanoverian forces commanded by the Duke of Cumberland.

One of the sons was the only Hanoverian

officer of distinction to be killed in the battle, while his brother, who commanded three squadrons of cavalry and later succeeded to the title of 4th Marquess of Lothian, later distinguished himself in Britain's wars with France.

In later centuries, as Britain stamped its imperial authority on the high seas, Sir Walter Talbot, a son of the 7th Marquess of Lothian, served the interests of the Empire as Admiral of the Fleet, a post he held from 1899 until 1904.

Other notable Kerrs have included the renowned book collector and 3rd Duke of Roxburgh, John Kerr (1740 – 1804), and the physicist John Kerr (1824-1907).

In the world of contemporary politics, Michael Andrew Foster Jude Kerr, better known under the rather less cumbersome name of Michael Ancram, is a distinguished Conservative Party politician, a former Advocate at the Scottish Bar, and the 13th Marquess of Lothian.

The Border=‑‑‑‑‑